My Own

Happiness

Journey

12-Step Program To Transform Your Life

Saghar Alavi

Published and Distributed in Canada by LLH Publishing Inc. www.andreaseydel.com

Library of Congress Cataloging-in-Publication Data

Alavi, Saghar
My Own Happiness Journey: A -12Step Program to Transform Your Life \ Saghar, Alavi
Nonfiction > Psychology > Mental Health
Nonfiction > Self-Help > Motivational & Inspirational
ISBN- 978-1-9991409-1-5
1st Printing: March 2019. Printed in Canada.
Design Credit: Yas Hassanzadeh
Editor: Farzad Amirmahani
Publisher's Note & Author DISCLAIMER

This publication is designed to provide accurate and authoritative information concerning the subject matter covered. It is sold with the understanding that the publisher and author are not engaging in or rendering any psychological, medical or other professional services. If expert assistance or counselling is needed, seek the services of a competent medical professional. For immediate support call your local crisis line. BE WELL.

LLH Publishing

Dedication

I dedicate this book to my mother who has lived a life full of positivity. She has been a role model and a symbol of resilience and happiness. She is capable of strongly going through challenges and facing them with bravery. My mom has taught me the importance of savouring life, and I cannot thank her enough for all her inspiration and
support.

Acknowledgements

I want to take this time to thank all my earth angels who have continually supported me throughout the journey of writing this book. Without their support, I would not have been able to complete this creation. To my husband who encourages and supports me every day, helping me believe in myself and take action. To my daughter who has taken so much care when designing this book. She has been a tremendous support although she is just a teenager. I am also very grateful for another wonderful angel put in my path by the universe, my writing coach, Andrea Seydel. Finally, and just as important, my sister, Khatereh who is always there for me and has been such a source of support and love.

Table of Contents

"Take time to make your soul happy."

By: Azita Ziaie

Your
JOURNEY
Starts Here!

Welcome to My Own Happiness Journey: A 12-Step Program to Transform Your Life! This is a transformative journal, designed to be a practical approach towards increasing your happiness and well-being. All the tools you need to enhance your happiness and resilience are found in the pages of this journal. With your dedication and work, you will find your own path towards optimal happiness. Since happiness means different things to different people, and it is more than just a smiley face, journaling and self-discovery are essential. By combining intentional behaviours with practice, you can improve your well-being.

Who is this journal for? If you have forgotten what happiness and overall well-being feels like, and you are unsure of how to shift things for the better, this journal is for you. If you are not clear yet on your own recipe for happiness, this journal offers the tools and strategies to support you along your journey. Lacking willpower? Feeling lost or broken? Are you not sure of where to start to make your life better? This journal is for you. If you have lots of unpracticed knowledge, but simply can't apply it, or you feel like there is a missing piece to the puzzle, you are going to love the gentle guidance of this journal.

The time is now, do not postpone your happiness. You can make happiness a priority with the help of this journal that takes you step by step through inner discovery, and provides you with the power to get where you want to go in life. This journal is a powerful tool that can train your mind for happiness and positivity in your life. Congratulations on starting to create your path towards your dream life. Throughout this book you will discover tools that are backed by scientific research, combined with your own personal effort, so you can create your own recipe for happiness. Get ready to discover your POWER and the HABITS you need to transform your life!

The mission of this journal is...

To help you find your own happiness so you can bounce back from challenges, and to make life easier for you, by providing you with step-by-step, guided inner discovery tools, that will help you journal combined with practical, science-based tips, creating your tailor-made happiness! After following this journal and doing the work, you will be able to make sustainable change, increase your happiness, flourish in your life, meet your maximum potential, create your dream life, participate in your future, build better relationships, and bounce back from whatever life throws at you.

The Power Of Journaling

Did you know that journaling is a useful therapeutic tool from which people of all ages can benefit? It is about writing freely whatever comes to your mind at that moment. There really isn't a right or wrong way to write in a journal. Keeping a diary is not the same thing as keeping a journal. With a diary, you primarily record daily occurrences and happenings in your life. With a journal, in contrast, you zone in on your reactions and perceptions, allowing you to dig deeper into events, occurrences, wishes, and dreams. Journaling is a wonderful tool that offers powerful insight and guidance for living your best life.

Journaling helps you gain clarity and insight into your world and your thinking. By writing in a journal you are better able to gain a new perspective and find meaning surrounding the circumstances of your life. You can also identify areas that require your attention or work. The art of journaling allows you to clarify thoughts and feelings, thereby acting as a tool for positive mental health. The act of writing in your journal gets your thinking out of your head and onto paper, which removes you one step, allowing you to gain new perspective.

It has been shown that there are health benefits that come with regular journaling as well. Researcher and psychologist, James Pennebaker from the University of Texas, discovered that regular journaling strengthens immune cells, and decreases asthma and rheumatoid arthritis symptoms. His studies also verify that writing about stressful events, and working through the thinking, act as a stress management tool, thus reducing the impact of life stressors on your physical health. Journaling has been proven to be a useful therapeutic tool. Writing about anger, sadness, and other painful emotions can help you work through these emotions, and discover what they are telling you. Journaling positive emotions like gratitude, kindness, or joy can have a positive effect on your emotional state.

Writing in a journal also encourages more mindfulness in your life. According to numerous studies, and Sonja Lyumbermirsky's 12 Strategies of Happiness, mindfulness increases our subjective well-being. Journaling is a powerful tool to bring you into a state of mindfulness; it helps bring you into the present moment, which helps you become more mindful about what is going on for you in your mind.

Journaling is a wonderful tool that requires self-discipline. Practicing the art of journaling, and setting aside the time to write, is an act of self-discipline. Like a muscle, the more you exercise self-regulation, the stronger it becomes. Habits formed in one area of your life have a tendency to spread. Since it has so many powerful benefits, the building of a journaling habit will benefit many areas of your life.

Not only does it help us be more mindful, journaling also allows us to track patterns and take notice of what is going on in our world. These could be negative thoughts and behaviours, or even positive strengths and learning opportunities. Journaling is essentially like a mental tracker, ready for our full investigation. By zeroing in on a problem or on opportunities, we can better manage and respond to our lives. The exercise of writing in a journal allows you to know yourself better. You will discover and get to know what makes you feel happy and confident. You will also gain clarity on situations and people that are toxic for you.

Journaling is also a powerful tool to help you solve conflicts more effectively, and resolve disagreements with others. Writing things down can create the space and perspective shift that we might need in order to solve problems or investigate options. There are so many powerful benefits to journaling. Let's get started on your own personal journey towards journaling and self-discovery, so you can make happiness a BIG part of your life.

1

Discovering Your Dreams

"Go confidently in the direction of your dreams! Live the life you've imagined."

-Thoreau

Discovering Your Dreams

To be truthful, many of us give up on our dreams, but dreaming big and connecting with your dream life can actually provide us with the fuel for growth, motivation, and success. Everything once started as a dream. Even the best inventions started with imagination, and a dream.

No dream is silly or unrealistic. Sometimes people give up on their dreams just because something goes against the mainstream, or runs in a different direction than the norm, but I am here to tell you that it doesn't mean that your dream is impossible! Quite the opposite. I invite you to dream again, to use the power of your dreams and your mind to live the best life for yourself. Ellen Johnson Sirleaf wrote: "If your dreams do not scare you, they are not big enough." It's time to get back to your dreams, or dream up some new, bigger dreams for yourself.

Your mind is powerful, and your dreams can provide you with the ability to focus, and drive you into action. Your dreams can come true. They also help in aiming towards a target. Dreaming of something that is important to you can change the direction of your day, and the course of your life. Dreams help you be motivated and inspired, and they will improve your life. Dreams are essentially thoughts you can see in your mind's eye.

Think of them as wishes for your life, and a way to help you gain deep focus. These are what will take you forward. This is the first step of your journey towards your happiest life. These dreams will help you realize the significance and importance of working towards making them come true. Your dreams are like a dress rehearsal for the life you desire for yourself.

Magic Sleep

Daria Shevtsova

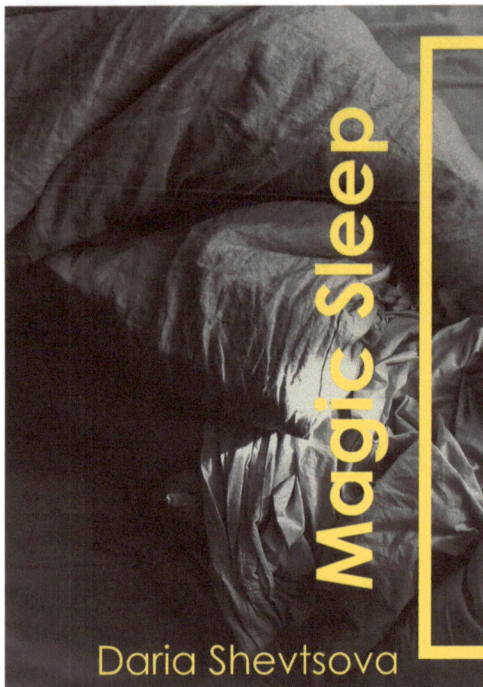

Can you imagine if a miracle happened overnight, while you were sleeping, and you woke up the next morning and your dreams came true? What would happen, and how would your life be different? JOURNAL THIS! Really use your imagination, and don't hold back on the details. Highlight the most important parts of this magical sleep that stands out most for you.

1. What do you love to learn about, or what skills have you always admired in others, but never tried for yourself?

2. What did you enjoy doing as a child?

3. Who are the five people that inspire you, and why?

4. What can you start to say yes to?

5. What could your life look like? If you made a collage, what would be in those images?

6. What don't you want? What do you want?

Write your insight here...

You're all about becoming your best self, but you're still not even sure what that looks like. Sometimes finding out what you actually want your life to look like is a daunting task. So, why even bother dreaming up a vision for yourself? Rest assured that you don't have to have life all planned out. Also, remember that it won't always come together exactly as we dream it up. But science shows it is beneficial and fun to have dreams to work towards. Can you even imagine your potential? Here are some tools you can use to define what you want in your dream life.

Six Question
to Ask Yourself to Figure Out Your Dream Life

Making a
Vission Board

What is a Dream/Vision Board?

A dream or vision board is a visualization tool which refers to a board or paper of any sort that is used to build a collage of words and pictures that represent your goals and dreams. The best way to achieve your goals is to keep them close to the top of your mind, as a constant reminder of what you desire. Place the finished product somewhere highly visible, so that it serves as a continual, visual reminder of where you want to be in the future. This way, you will always be looking for ways to move yourself closer to your goals. A dream or vision board is a wonderful tool to help you visualize the future you desire for yourself. By adding this visual practice to your daily routine, you will naturally become more excited to move in the direction of your dream life, and reach your goals. You'll start to notice you are unexpectedly doing things that move you closer to your ideal life.

How to create your Dream/Vision Board?

Have fun with the process. There is no right or wrong way to create this board. Find pictures that best represent or symbolize the big dreams you want to attract into your life, and place them on your board. You can even create a document on your computer, cut and paste images onto the document, and have it printed. I love this technique, as you can print multiple copies. Have fun with the process! Be creative. You can include images and words, or anything that really represents your dreams. Make sure you have a really good representation of your ideal future. My tip is to make a list of your goals, or what you'd like to achieve, in order to be in the head space to visualize your dreams accomplished. Then create your vision/dream board from that list. Take moments every day to look over your vision board, and keep it where you can see it often. I love keeping mine beside my bed at night. Keep a date on your vision board, and notice how baby steps happen in your life that prove you are moving towards your big dreams. Print or create extra copies. Keep a copy here in this journal if you can. Remember to use this dream board as inspiration and proof that your life is moving in the right direction. Use it as daily motivation and guidance. Feel yourself living your best life as you look at the images, and act as if you have already achieved these goals.

"If you can dream it, you can do it."

- Walt Disney

Reflection

What was your biggest discovery through this step?

How are you going to bring this practice into your life?

How will this contribute to your life?

2

Goal
Setting

"Follow your dreams, believe in yourself and don't give up"

-Rachel Corrie

Goal Setting

The Difference Between Goals and Dreams

Dreams and goals work hand in hand. Many people endeavour to reach dreams, but fail to set goals. Both dreams and goals exist in the mind; however, what distinguishes a dream from a goal is the fact that the latter has a planned and determined deadline. You can see how dreams and goals need to work together. The first step to create a goal is to have a clear vision of your dream. In addition to the desired result, a goal includes plans and commitments that will ensure the fruitfulness of the ambition.

This means that you can't just sit on the couch all day in your sweats dreaming of owning your own business and call that a goal. You need to get up and do something about it. It is important to understand that the journey to setting and achieving your goals will not all be smooth sailing. Be prepared to face naysayers and other obstacles. The most important concept is to never lose sight of what you are working for and why. Be fearless and chase the dream with all the confidence you have. If you dream and believe it, you can make it happen by setting goals.

Why Set Goals?

Successful people and achievers in all fields set goals. Setting goals gives you long-term vision and short-term motivation. It helps you focus on what you want, and organize your time and resources so that you can make the most of your life.

Spend some time brainstorming your dreams, and then select one or more goals in each category of your life that best reflect(s) what you want to do.

Top reasons to create and set goals:
- Forms a clear path and a sense of control over your life
- Gives you the ability to focus on your day and activities
- Produces a sense of accountability and motivates you
- Allows you to dream big and strive for greater things
- Helps you see the long-term vision of your future

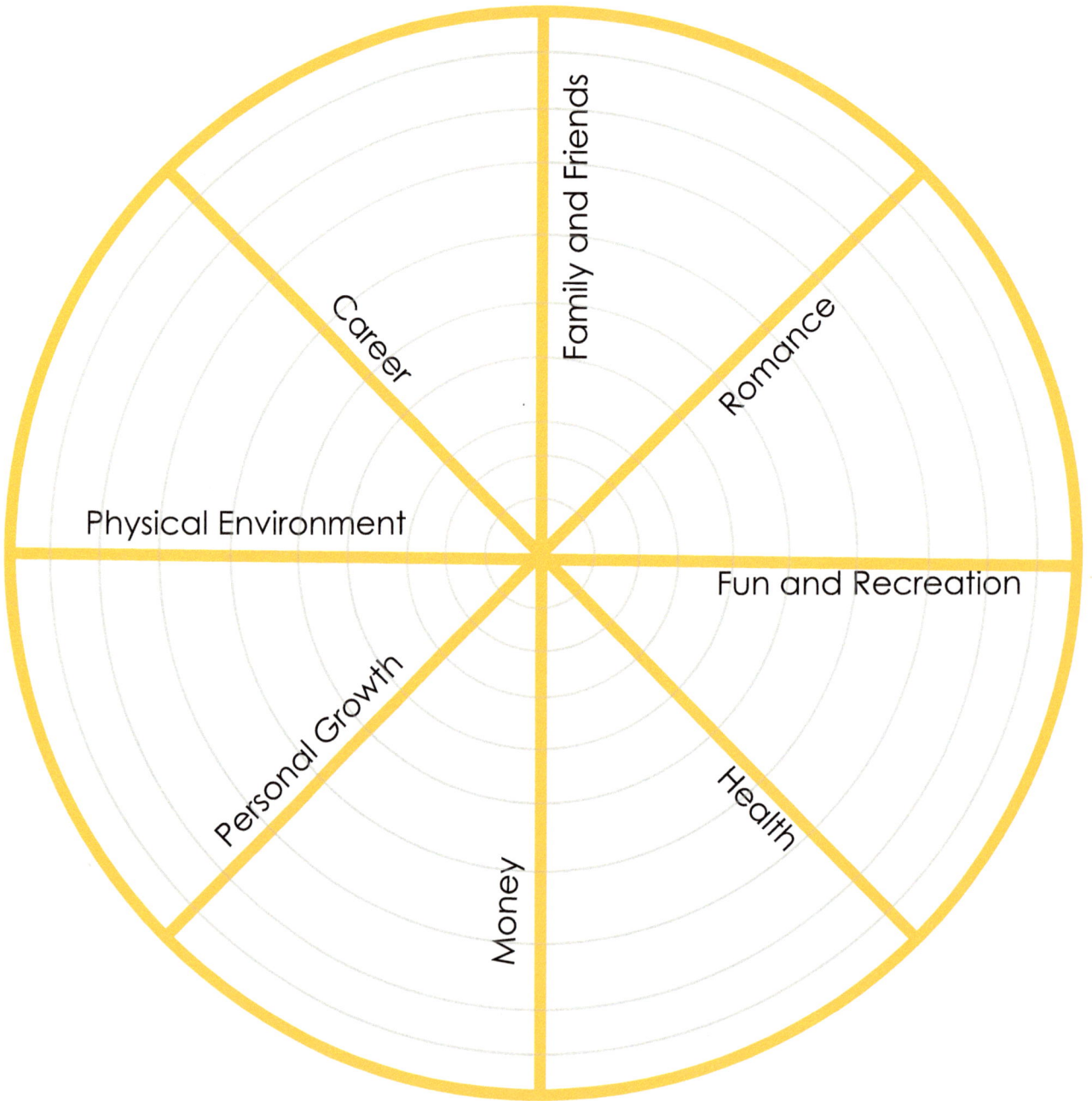

Family and Friends

Romance

Career

Physical Environment

Fun and Recreation

Personal Growth

Health

Money

This wheel contains eight sections that, together, represent one way of describing a whole life. The exercise measures your level of satisfaction in these eight areas of your life on the day you work through this exercise. It shows you what balance in your life looks like. This is a great tool to help you see what goals you could make for yourself for each of these areas in your life.

Directions: The eight sections in the Wheel of Life represent different aspects of your life. Seeing the centre of the wheel as 1 (lowest), and the outer edges as 10 (highest), rank your level of satisfaction with each life area by drawing a straight or curved line to create a new outer edge. The new perimeter represents the wheel of your life. If this were an actual wheel, how bumpy would the ride be? Based on your ratings, journal what area of your life requires more attention. What goals could you set for yourself moving forward that would help bring you more balance?

Vission Board

Top Priority Goals

Based on your results from both the Wheel of Life and the upcoming value exercises, make a master goal list for yourself here. Take your list of goals and determine which ones need your undivided focus at this time. Which ones excite you the most? What is/are your top goal(s), you desire most for yourself right now? Which one(s) do you want to commit to for the next chapter in your life?

Write your insight here...

Write your insight here...

What Do You Value?

Having a clear sense of what you value can help you when formulating your goals. Making sure that your goals support what you value and life purpose will feed your soul and contribute to your happiness. Take time to think about and note 3-5 times in your life when you were most proud of yourself. What difference did you make, and what impact did you have on others? Then, notice any common threads mixed throughout your stories. These are things that you value, and what brings meaning to your life. Narrow down your list to the top 3-5 things that you value! For example: I value learning. I value connections. I value teaching.

Circle which values matter to you most.

Creativity	Balance	Religion	Enthusiasm
Fairness	Knowledge	Respect	Generosity
Faith	Leadership	Self-respect	Power
Friendships	Learning	Success	Intelligence
Adventure	Love	Perseverance	Patience
Fun	Loyalty	Confidence	Obedience
Happiness	Openness	Determination	Bravery
Honesty	Optimism	Diversity	Fitness
Humour	Peace	Resilience	Punctuality

Reflection

What was your biggest discovery through this step?

How are you going to bring this practice into your life?

How will this contribute to your life?

3

Action Plan

"Don't wait until you are ready to take action. Instead, take action to be ready."

-Jensen Siaw

Action Plan

What's an Action Plan

Whether it's sending out an email newsletter, putting together a presentation, or working on a book for a publisher, many of us have to complete simple projects as part of our day-to-day responsibilities. These small to medium-sized projects may, at first glance, not seem to need much thought. But, occasionally, we can overlook a key step or "to do" item that can derail all our efforts.

For instance, how do you make sure that you've covered everything? Are there any actions that need to be taken early on in the project for it to succeed? Are you clear about when you need to do key tasks, and in what sequence, to meet your deadline? Action plans are simple lists of all of the tasks that you need to finish to meet an objective or a goal.

They are different than to-do lists in that they focus on the achievement of a single goal. Action plans are useful because they give you a framework for thinking about how you'll complete a project efficiently. They help you finish activities in a sensible order, and they help you ensure that you don't miss any key steps. Also, because you can see each task laid out, you can quickly decide which tasks you'll outsource, and which tasks you may be able to disregard. Action planning has a number of specific advantages over a list of things to do, or scheduling work using a calendar or diary:

- It provides an opportunity for reflection. Before beginning something, it is helpful to think about what is involved with completing a goal.
- It clarifies the objective. It is a great opportunity to get clarity on what needs to be done.
- It builds focus. It allows for you to have a laser-like focus on the task at hand. It also increases your ability to prioritize your life appropriately. When you are focused, it is easier for important actions to emerge.

• It creates ownership and accountability. When you make an action plan, you are more likely to follow through to task completion. The involvement process creates a sense of ownership and motivation. It also allows you to take notice of how well you are progressing, or if you are progressing at all!

• It clarifies timescales. Setting out all the tasks that need to be done to achieve a particular objective, and making decisions about how much resource is available for each task, allows for a realistic assessment of how long the overall action plan will take. Every action in an action plan should have a clear completion date.

• It identifies measures of success. Measures of success are like stepping stones towards a larger objective. They provide a way of measuring progress towards your goal. This process creates a sense of ownership and motivation. It also allows you to take notice of how well you are, or are not, progressing.

An action plan is a tool that can help you identify:

- the steps that must be taken to reach a goal
- In what order to take these action steps
- who might be able to take some of these steps for you
- what resources you might need to accomplish your tasks
- what outcome and timeline you desire

Plan here!

"Personal power is the ability to take action."

-Anthony Robbins

Mind The Gap

Thomas Craig

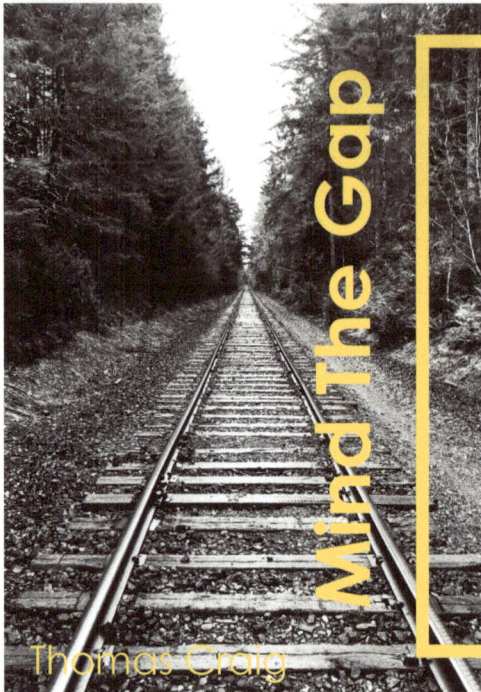

In her book Daring Greatly, Brené Brown suggests that we mind the gap, paying attention to where we are now, and where we would like to be. Take your list of goals and where you would like to be, and notice the gap between them. The space between where you currently are, and where your goal lies, requires a strategy and an action plan. Ask yourself these powerful questions in order to "dare greatly": What do you want to achieve? Why you do want to reach this goal? How are you going to get there? Think about the goals you want to accomplish and the steps you need to take to be successful.

Write your insight here...

Write your insight here...

Write an
Action Plan

To draw up an action plan, simply list the tasks that you need to carry out to achieve your goal, in the order that you need to complete them. Specify which goal you would like to achieve, then go through each step here to progressively realize your goals. Start by brainstorming all of the tasks that you need to complete in order to accomplish your goal. Think step by step what you need to do. Organize your list and start to look at your list in order of priorities or sequence. Create a MASTER ACTION PLAN list and make due dates for each action item. Make a plan and the order in which to take steps. Then start knocking off the items, and incorporate the action plan into your daily, weekly, and monthly planner. Reward your hard work. To remian fully motivated, it is essential to plan to reward yourself along the journey towards your goals. Take each of your goals, along with your action plan, and decide what and where you can apply rewards.

"The distance between your dreams and reality is called action."

-Unknown

Reflection

What was your biggest discovery through this step?

How are you going to bring this practice into your life?

How will this contribute to your life?

4

Energizing Life Skills

"Self-care means giving yourself permission to pause."

-Cecilia Tran

Energizing Life Skills

What is self care?

Self-care is important for your physical health, as well as your mental, spirtual, and overall health. Without self-care, your relationships with others, your ability to reach your dreams, and your subjective well-being can suffer. Self-care is a broad term that encompasses just about anything you do to be good to yourself. In a nutshell, it's about being as kind to yourself as you would be to others.

It's partly about knowing when your resources are running low, and stepping back to replenish them, rather than letting them all drain away. Self-care is important, but some people think it's selfish or inconsiderate. Science shows that it is essential for our well-being. We know self-care actually makes you more effective and energetic.

When you avoid things that make you feel physically and mentally well, you deplete your level of confidence and self-esteem. Self-care is important to maintain a healthy relationship with yourself, and is sometimes called self-love. It means different things to different people, but overall it is the ability to care for yourself, in order to show up in your life as best as you can.

Energizing Benefits of Self Care

It produces positive feelings, which in turn, improve confidence, motivation, and energy levels. The best way to do this, is to implement small but important self-care habits every day. As it turns out, there are many different self-care practices, and not all of them suit everyone. Self-care also involves integrating self-compassion into your life in a way that helps prevent even the possibility of burnout.

As aforementioned, there are many benefits of self-care. The most obvious relates to mood and energy levels. However, research shows wider ranging benefits as well.

Better productivity. When you learn how to say "no" to things that over-extend you and start making time for things that matter more, you slow life down in a wonderful way. This brings your goals into sharper focus and helps you concentrate on what is important to you.

Improved immune system. There is evidence that most self-care activities activate your parasympathetic nervous system (PNS). What this means is that your body goes into a restful, rejuvenating mode, helping it fortify its immune system.

Enhanced self-esteem. When you regularly carve out time that's only about being good to yourself and meeting your own needs, you send a positive message to your subconscious. In other words, by treating yourself like you matter and have intrinsic value, you can drastically improve your self-esteem.

Increased self-knowledge. Practicing self-care requires thinking about what you really love to do. The exercise of figuring out what makes you feel passionate and inspired can help you understand yourself a lot better. Sometimes, this can even spark a change in career, or a reprioritization of previously abandoned hobbies.

More to give. When you're good to yourself, you might think you're being selfish. In truth, self-care gives you the resources you need to be compassionate and giving to others as well. Giving compassion and kindness to others is a bit like filling a bucket; you can't fill someone else's if you don't have enough of your own! You've heard the expression: "You can't pour from an empty cup."

Top reasons why self-care is not selfish:
- It helps you be authentic and a better person for others.
- You can help others only once you have taken care of yourself.
- Self-care connects you to your purpose and allows you to show up in your life in such a way that makes a bigger impact.
- You will become more motivated, recharged and feel worthy of amazing things.

Self-care isn't just important; it's crucial.

"You can't pour from an empty cup. Take care of yourself first."

-Unknown

Self Care Checklist

This is a simple checklist that has been scientifically shown to offer self-care. Be sure to do some or all of these things, often. Add your own to the list with the next exercise.

O Make a date with yourself: Spend an hour alone doing something that nourishes you.
O Praise the process you've already taken when you do something awesome.
O Listen to music and sing along.
O Read books that inspire you.
O Unplug.
O Paint or write.
O Learn something new.
O Meditate.
O Take a new, fun class.
O Get in touch with your values and spirituality.
O Take a nap (a 20-minute replenisher).
O Be mindful.
O Laugh.
O Eat healthy food.
O Make a grateful list.
O Have a sauna or bath.
O Do something just because it makes you happy.
O Be kind to someone.
O Declutter your home.
O Drink plenty of water.
O Do yoga stretches.
O Run or walk.
O Calm your mind.
O Enjoy pets.
O Take deep breaths of fresh air.
O Sit in nature.
O Spend time with friends.
O Go to bed early.

SELF-CARE STARTER KIT

Create a list of self-care activities you can complete in 15 minutes (or longer) for each section below. Think about activities you can do that would feed and energize you! Use your list as a starting point to add more self-care into your life! Capture activities that fuel, recharge, and nurture you:

MIND

BODY

SPIRIT

CREATIVITY

Mindfulness. What exactly is it, why should we be mindful, and how mindfulness exercises actually work? Mindfulness is acknowledging the present for what it is, and focusing on being in the moment. It seems simple in theory, but how often do you find yourself with a spare minute to stop, breathe, and ruminate on life? Remember to breathe. First up is breathing. It's very much an essential part of life and, believe it or not, there are many ways you can do it. Deep breathing slows the heart rate, increases the flow of oxygenated blood to the brain, and calms the mind. One breathing technique that aids in soothing and slowing stress is the 4-7-8 exercise: Exhale completely from the mouth with a whoosh sound; inhale through the nose to the count of 4; hold this breath for 7 seconds; exhale again with a whooshing breath to the count of 8. This technique is excellent for relaxing the body, and clearing the mind, and you're guaranteed to feel calm and recharged after this exercise. In a similar way to breathing, meditation is the true embodiment of mindfulness. Meditation is a powerful tool, and requires setting aside time to focus solely on you. To meditate is to reflect inwardly. If you are new to meditation there are many online meditation resources to try. It is an excellent way to not only eliminate stress and anxiety, but to become a happier and more positive person.

Three Good Things

Reflection is the time you take to really think carefully about life's moments. Whether you reflect internally, or you choose to journal, reflection —like meditation—is taking some time to sit back and accept things for what they are. Once we are able to reflect and accept, we can move past negative thoughts. A great exercise is writing daily about THREE GOOD THINGS that we are grateful for in our lives. Write down three good things:

"Self-care is giving the world the best of you instead of what's left of you."

-Katie Reed

Reflection

What was your biggest discovery through this step?

How are you going to bring this practice into your life?

How will this contribute to your life?

5

Habits & Rituals

"You will never change your life until you change something you do daily."

-John C. Maxwell

Habits and Rituals

A habit is a routine of behaviour that is repeated regularly and tends to occur subconsciously. It is routine, in that our brain has created neural networks (pathways) in order to repeat the behaviour without needing to consciously think about it. Habits and routines are meant to make our lives easier.

Habitual behaviour often goes unnoticed in people who exhibit it because a person does not need to engage in self-analysis when undertaking routine tasks. New behaviours can become automatic through the process of habit formation. Old habits are hard to break, and new ones are hard to form because the behavioural patterns which humans repeat become imprinted in neural pathways. A ritual is something done repeatedly with a purpose outside of the action itself. Rituals can be very useful when trying to create new habits. In the process of forming a habit, people can rely on rituals to adopt the new habit.

Habits are the basis of your success—or maybe your downfall. Habits are often thought of negatively, such as a drug habit or a gambling habit, but there can be good habits, such as exercising regularly, making thoughtful comments, meditating, thinking hard about research topics, and starting projects long before deadlines. A habit is something we do regularly without consciously thinking much about it. It is an automatic mental and behavioural activity. Habits make it possible for us to do things without expending huge amounts of mental effort. They make everyday life possible— for good or bad. Charles Duhigg sets forth his findings about habits in his book, The Power of Habit: Why We Do What We Do in Life and Business (Random House, 2012). Developing a habit of daily deliberate practice towards our goals is the most important thing to be learned. Habits become essential parts of our success and goal meeting. Duhigg establishes that there are three key elements in a habit loop: a cue or trigger to initiate a behaviour, a routine behaviour, and a reward.

You might be asking, "So how do I change my bad habits? How do I stop overeating, and start exercising? How do I stop procrastinating, and start working on my important long-term projects?" Duhigg says you need to do some practical investigation to find out what the cues are for your habits, and what actions you can use to replace your routine behaviour.

Implementation Intention Statement

Your habits matter because you become your habits. Commit to your new habits with the implementation intention strategy used in positive psychology. This is where you put your plan into strategy. This statement you create will ensure you implement your desired action. It's like a plan for when, where and how you plan to execute your new habit. For instance:

During the next week, I will participate in at least 20 minutes of exercise on (DAY) at (TIME) in (PLACE).

Make your own implementation intention statement:

"We are what we repeatedly do. Excellence, then, is not an act, but a habit."

-Aristotle

Tiny Changes

In the book Atomic Habits, James Clear, one of the world's leading experts on habit formation, reveals practical strategies that will teach us exactly how to master the tiny behaviours that will lead to remarkable results!

IDENTIFY:
What do you want to be? What habits and rituals will support the person you want to become?

BUILD:
Build better habits that will support your goals. Tiny changes make a big difference.

PLAN:
Create a daily system that supports your new desired habits.

Strategies for Habits and Rituals

The best way to make a permanent change is to focus on daily, incremental improvements. The key here is to make slow changes to your life. It will all add up to eventual permanent change to your life. Great results are built from small actions that you take every day. Here are some strategies to help you.

Strategies:

First, you can identify your current habits and routines. Then decide what new habits and routines you desire. In positive psychology, there is a term called "ego depletion," which basically means your willpower has a limited amount of energy every day. Focus on one habit at a time. In a way, willpower is like a muscle. It can get tired and worn out from overuse. Keep exercising your willpower to make it stronger. Find an accountability partner, or seek a professional life coach to be a part of your support system. Create incentives and set rewards for each new habit.

Put these strategies into practice:
1. Identify your habit routine (pick only one).
2. Break it down into CUE-ROUTINE-REWARD.
- What behaviour do you want to replace/change?
- What could be a new routine?
- What could be a new reward?
3. Identify who you can call on for help and accountability.
4. Set up your planned rewards for habit change.

Creating Rituals

If you want to incorporate more routine and structure into your life, creating rituals and routines is essential to start and create new habit loops. You might struggle to follow a routine if you are disorganized or distracted, if you procrastinate, or set unrealistic goals, if you are a perfectionist, or if you have poor time management. What are your own struggles? Once you've identified your main problem areas, and realized what's stopping you from becoming a more productive and habitual individual, you will know where to start making changes. It is amazing how small daily habits or actions can contribute to the life we desire for ourselves. When you create routines, rituals and actions, you form new habits that will fuel your day. After all, in the words of Aristotle, "We are what we repeatedly do."

MORNING RITUALS:
What could your morning rituals or routines look like?
What could you do to your environment to support new habits and form rituals? What morning rituals can set your day up for success?
Some examples could be: making your bed, saying a prayer for the day, pulling an inspirational card, or savouring your tea or coffee.
What can your morning rituals and routines be?

Design and plan them here!

BEDTIME RITUALS:

What could your evening rituals or routines look like?

Since it is the end of the day, it is a wonderful time to reflect and close your day in a positive way. You can also take this time to prepare for the next day. What routines or rituals would you like to add to your bedtime?

Are there some forms of self-care that you could incorporate into your bedtime ritual that would feel nourishing?

Are there any things you could do to prepare for the next day?

What could you do to reflect on your day and celebrate the person you are?

Some examples could be: lighting a candle, writing in your journal, saying a prayer, cleansing your face while saying affirmations, deep breathing exercises, or meditation.

What can your bedtime rituals and routines be?

Design and plan them here!

Set Up Keystone Habits

Charles Duhigg, the author of The Power of Habit, talks about keystone habits. Keystone habits are the ones that create and start a chain effect in your life that produce a number of positive outcomes. The development of keystone habits can become a critical part of your personal journey of development. Keystone habits are correlated with other good habits. For example, at first you wanted more physical activity, but this keystone habit generated a number of additional habits; regular exercise often goes hand-in-hand with better eating habits. Another example might be waking up early every morning. Your initial goal is to wake up early, but waking up early can lead to other positive habits that you were not intending on having such as: being more productive in your day, fitting in exercise, having more time for family, and having more energy.

Here are seven examples of effective keystone habits that can have a ripple effect on your life:

1. Exercise
2. Sleep
3. Meditation
4. Waking up early
5. Visualization
6. Journaling
7. Drinking more water

What are your possible keystone habits? List them here...

Reflection

What was your biggest discovery through this step?

How are you going to bring this practice into your life?

How will this contribute to your life?

6

Intimacy & Connections

"Feeling connected to each other is a basic human need."

-Martin Seligman

Intimacy and Connections

what are social connections and intimacy?

Social connections improve health, well-being and longevity. Social connectedness is the measure of how people come together and interact. It involves the quality and number of connections an individual has with other people. These connections can be the social circle of family, friends, and acquaintances. Social groups are an important part of our identity and they teach us skills that help us run our daily lives. This human connection brings value to our lives. Relationships bring us a sense of belonging and act as a therapeutic support system.

why are connections and intimacy important?

As Emma Seppälä, the author of The Happiness Track says, "We all know the basics of health 101: Eat your veggies, go to the gym and get proper rest. But how many of us know that social connections are as important? Social connections improve physical health and psychological well-being." Numerous studies have shown that a lack of social connections affects our health and leads to a greater chance of obesity, smoking, high blood pressure, and depression. Social connections have shown to increase longevity as well as contribute to social and emotional psychological well-being. Bottom line, science has shown that feelings of isolation, loneliness and alienation are not good for our health and well-being. Brené Brown, a professor at the University of Houston Graduate College of Social Work, specializes in social connection. In an interview, she said: "A deep sense of love and belonging is an irresistible need of all people. We are biologically, cognitively, physically, and spiritually wired to love, to be loved, and to belong. When those needs are not met, we don't function as we are meant to. We break. We fall apart. We numb. We ache. We hurt others. We get sick."

As well stated by Brené Brown, we are profoundly social creatures. But, as psychologists from Maslow to Baumeister have repeatedly stressed, the truth of the matter is that a sense of social connection and intimacy is one of our fundamental human needs. We need people and connections in our lives in order to be happy.

"Intimacy is not purely physical; it's the act of connecting with someone so deeply, you feel like you can see into their soul."

-Reshall Varsos

Fostering Friendships

While developing and maintaining friendships takes time and effort, according to the Harvard Health Publishing, good friends can improve your mood. Spending time with positive friends can elevate your mood, boost your outlook, and help you to reach your goals. Whether you're trying to get fit, give up smoking, or otherwise improve your life, encouragement from a friend can really boost your willpower, increase your chances of success and alleviate your stress and depression. Having an active social life can bolster your immune system, help reduce isolation (a major contributing factor to depression), and support you through tough times. Even if it's just having someone to share your problems with, friends can help you cope with serious illness, the loss of a job or loved one, the break-up of a relationship, or any other challenges in life. Friends can also support you when you get older. As you age, retirement, illness, and the death of loved ones can often leave you isolated. Having people whom you can turn to for company and support can provide purpose and be a buffer against depression, disability, hardship and loss. Boost your self-worth. Friendship is a two-way street, and the "give" side of the give-and-take contributes to your own sense of self-worth. Being there for your friends makes you feel needed and adds purpose to your life.

Journal here. Ask yourself:
Who are your closest friends?
When was the last time you talked to them?
When was the last time you saw them?

Creating New Friendships

Get out there!

Be friendlier and more social.

It can feel uncomfortable to put yourself out there socially, but you don't have to be naturally outgoing or live a life of perennial partying to make new friends.

Set intentions to create new friendships!

Be interested in others: The best way to connect with others is to be genuinely interested in them. Be curious and ask questions to get to know people. Listen more than you talk. Give undivided attention. In this day and age, there are many potential distractions, so it is important to give people your full, uncompromised attention. Pay close attention to what others are talking about. Try to interact, and reflect back based on what you notice. Remember what people say by paying close attention. See potential in acquaintances; you never know who could turn into one of your best friends. Be open to talking with people and turn some acquaintances into friends. Take the initiative to talk more and spend some time together.

TAKE THE MEET-A-NEW-FRIEND CHALLENGE:

When looking to meet new people, try to be open to new experiences. Not everything you try will be successful, but you can always learn from the experience and hopefully have some fun and meet new people. Set the intention to make new connections.

WHERE TO START:

Volunteer, take a class, join a club, walk your dog to the dog park, attend a show, join events, take moments to spark up conversation, frequent your local coffee shop, join group fitness classes, unplug and reach out, talk to a neighbour, reach out to previous acquaintances, track down and reach out to people on social media, carpool, add it to the calendar, create a group, be a friend, etc.

New Friend Challenge

In their book, The Seven Principles for Making Marriage Work, John Gottman and Nan Silver talk about the "Magic Five Hours," a series of happiness habits that can help your relationships. Gradually make each of the following suggestions a routine part of your relationships:

Take two minutes every weekday morning before leaving for work, school, or wherever you are going, and learn something about what your partner is doing during their day.

Take twenty minutes when you get home to decompress a little together before you get into an evening routine. Listen actively to your partner, and be supportive. Think twice before you start offering advice at this time—the goal is to listen.

Take five minutes every day to show a little appreciation and admiration. Practice gratitude towards your partner. Every single day, find something you appreciate about your partner. Give a genuine expression of how grateful you are for having your partner.

Take five minutes every day to give affection. Gottman and Silver suggest that you show affection through kissing, touching, holding, hugging, and closeness to your partner for at least five minutes a day.

Set aside two hours each week to get to know your partner better. Play games where you ask each other questions, or use the time to resolve a problem. If you don't have time or can't afford to go on a date, be creative: enjoy a glass of wine in the living room after the kids are in bed, or plan a date night to go for a walk together.

Quality Time

"To have someone understand your mind is a different kind of intimacy."

-Unknown

Reflection

What was your biggest discovery through this step?

How are you going to bring this practice into your life?

How will this contribute to your life?

7

Kindness & Forgiveness

"We rise by lifting others."

-Robert Ingersoll

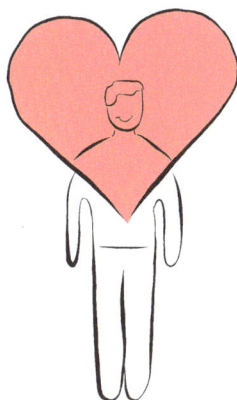

Kindness and Forgiveness

Being kind to others does make you happier. According to Psychology Today, researchers conclude that being kind to others causes a small, but significant improvement in subjective well-being. Performing random acts of kindness has been proven to be a way of boosting your mood. Doing good makes you feel good, and it also benefits others. But as you have probably already experienced, we don't need science to know that it feels good, to both give and receive kindness. Studies have found that the act of forgiveness can bring huge rewards for your health by lowering the risk of heart attack, improving cholesterol levels, and sleep, as well as reducing pain, blood pressure, levels of anxiety, depression, and stress. Gandhi once said, "Forgiveness is an attribute of the strong." It takes a lot of courage to move on from a painful experience inflicted on you by someone else. But if you do let go of that anger, you'll be bettering yourself in more ways than one. Hurt, anger, and disappointment all take a toll on both your mental and physical health, but forgiveness is a form of protection from these stresses. "There is an enormous physical burden to being hurt and disappointed," says Karen Swartz, M.D., director of the Mood Disorders Adult Consultation Clinic at The Johns Hopkins Hospital. This might be because forgiving people adopt better coping skills when they feel stressed, or their bodies may actually respond less to the negative event. "If you have a tendency to hang on to grudges you can train yourself out of it," Swartz says. It's your choice: do you want to dwell on hurts, or try to see the good in others?

Why and how does kindness make us happier?

There is power in a smile. Did you know that studies in neuroscience suggest that seeing someone else show an emotion automatically activates the same areas of the brain as if we experienced that emotion for ourselves? Think about it. If you see someone smile, doesn't that make you smile? It literally is contagious. Being kind is likely to make someone else smile! Simply by being kind we open the door to many opportunities for human connections.

"We rise by lifting others."

-Robert Ingersoll

Acts Of Kindness

How amazing would it be if we all did one small act of kindness each day? There are many resources online to find examples of acts of kindness. Make your own list in your journal. Check the list often. Notice what acts of kindness you practiced today, and what you might do tomorrow.

Here is a sample start to your list:
1. Leave money on a vending machine for someone.
2. Bake cookies for someone.
3. Volunteer for a few hours at a food bank.
4. Do a five-kilometer run or walk for a good cause.
5. Help out at an office.
6. Pick up litter on the beach.
7. Let someone go in front of you in line.
8. Give a stranger a compliment.
9. Make dinner for a family in need.
10. Insert coins into someone's parking meter.
11. Buy flowers to hand out on the street.
12. Leave letters of encouragement on people's cars.
13. Buy a movie ticket for the person behind you.
14. Pay for someone's meal at a restaurant.
15. Write letters or text messages to people who might be lonely.
16. Donate Christmas gifts.
17. Participate in a fundraiser.
18. Use your allowance to donate to a charity.
19. Hold open the doors for people.
20. Thank people with a random gift.

Journal your KINDNESS ideas:

Take these steps towards forgiveness:

1. Start by making a list of all the people you feel have hurt you in some way.

2. Pick the person that has hurt you the least from this list. Start there.

3. Think about what has been particularly challenging about this person.

4. Write out the reason this person has negatively impacted your life. If you need to, decide and acknowledge what this person has done is not okay, then allow yourself to feel the emotions that arise for you.

5. At this point make a decision to forgive this person. You are not condoning the challenging behaviours but you are choosing to forgive. This will give you the opportunity to free yourself from the mental stress or pain.

6. Start to offer understanding, compassion and empathy towards this person. What wounds or challenges have they potentially been dealing with? What might be going on for them in their life that is challenging? Compassion and understanding other people's perspectives sometimes makes it easier to forgive others.

7. Think or say out loud, "I forgive you."

8. Is there anything that you want to learn from this situation? Are there any new boundaries that you need to set for yourself?

9. REPEAT these steps with each person that you have listed.

Forgiveness

Forgiveness Letter

You can try making a new ritual for yourself: Write a letter to the person who has upset you, expressing your hurt and anger. Then, burn that letter (safely), and write another letter expressing forgiveness. You may choose to send the second letter, or not, but thinking out your own reasons for forgiving will help protect you mentally and physically. Where you allow your mind to go during this exercise is the most important thing to take from it. So, by letting go and forgiving, you will be able to put your mind onto different, more positive things.

Forgive Yourself Meditation

Forgiveness does not mean condoning, forgetting, or excusing bad behaviour, nor does it mean denying or minimizing your own feelings. It simply means that you no longer dwell on those feelings.

1) Find yourself a comfortable posture, or take a moment lying on the floor, or a bed.

2) Bring your attention to the physical sensation of breathing, notice whatever is pulling at your attention, or whatever you're feeling now, and without judgment, bring your attention back to the rising and falling of your breath.

3) Bring to mind anything that you judge yourself for. Maybe you feel regret, irritation, or sadness. Notice how it feels even bringing it to mind. Then focus on these three phrases, not forcing anything, but setting an intention: I forgive myself for not understanding. I forgive myself for making mistakes. I forgive myself for causing pain and suffering to myself and others.

4) Bring your attention back again and repeat the phrases. For a few moments instead of focusing on your breath, use these phrases as the focus of your attention.

Journal anything that comes up for you. This type of practice may become too painful. At any time, without judging yourself, come back and focus on your breathing. Allow yourself to settle and return when you're ready, now or maybe some time in the future. Forgiveness doesn't mean being passive or not taking action. It doesn't mean standing down when we need to protect ourselves or someone else from harm.

Reflection

What was your biggest discovery through this step?

How are you going to bring this practice into your life?

How will this contribute to your life?

8

Gratitude & Spirituality

"If you want to find happiness,
find gratitude."

-Steve Maraboli

Gratitude and Spirituality

Gratitude is an emotion similar to appreciation that most people are familiar with. Gratitude has many benefits in terms of our health, happiness, satisfaction with life, and the way we relate to others. Science has shown that gratitude can improve our health, relationships, emotions, personality, and career. Gratitude makes us feel more gratitude, in other words, gratitude triggers positive feedback loops. We, as humans, have what is called hedonic adaptation, where after repeated exposure to the same emotion-producing stimulus, we tend to experience less of that emotion. In other words, we get use to the good things that happen to us. Unfortunately, due to hedonic adaptation, we stop seeing as much positive and start complaining. If we want to maximize our happiness, gratitude is one of the most powerful tools in our arsenal. It makes the good times "stickier" and more memorable. Cultivating gratitude is a skill. Gratitude makes us nicer, more trusting, more social, and more appreciative. As a result, it helps us make more friends, deepen our existing relationships, and improve our marriages. Gratitude reduces feelings of envy, makes our memories happier, lets us experience good feelings, and helps us bounce back from stress. Gratitude is also strongly correlated with optimism. Optimism, in turn, makes us happier, improves our health, and our relationships. Spirituality is more of an individual practice, and has to do with having a sense of peace and purpose in life. It also relates to the process of developing beliefs around the meaning of life and connection with others. Happy people generally experience pleasurable emotions, but also identify their lives as meaningful. They tend to feel they contribute in some way to their community and that they have an effect on the world around them. Since spirituality is so deeply rooted in providing meaning, it becomes an access point for greater happiness. That is, the more spiritual you are, the more likely you are to be grateful. Spirituality helps people identify their values and appreciate the same values in others. Many spiritual traditions encourage belonging to a community. Such a sense of belonging promotes relationships and connections, and is clearly one of the highest indicators of a happy life.

"Enjoy the little things, for one day you may look back and realize they were the BIG THINGS."

-Robert Brault

Thank You Letter

Write a thank-you note. You can make yourself happier, and nurture your relationship with another person by writing a thank-you letter expressing your enjoyment and appreciation of that person's impact on your life. Send it, or better yet, deliver and read it in person if possible. Make a habit of sending at least one gratitude letter a month. Once in a while, write one to yourself.

Who can you write thank-you notes to?

Meditation

Meditation can be done any time of day. You decide when the best time is for you. Meditation contributes to a sense of peace and clarity. Any time you meditate you will reap the benefits. There is beauty and simplicity in meditation because you don't need any equipment to do it. All that's required is a quiet space and a few minutes each day. Preferably, meditate at the same time every morning; that way you'll establish the habit. Pretty soon you'll always meditate in the morning, just like brushing your teeth.

Step 1: Set aside a place to meditate.

Step 2: Sit comfortably in a chair or on the floor with your back straight. Close your eyes.

Step 3: Begin to breathe slowly, deeply, and gently. Keep your mind focused inwardly or on your breath. If it wanders, gently steer it back to focus. Your breath is your life source. Make a commitment to being more conscious of your breath. Recognize that within this breath you are connected to the energy of all creation, that you are a part of it, and that it is always a part of you.

Step 4: You can continue to focus on your breath and simply stay with that, or shift your meditation to expressions of gratitude:

I am thankful for my health.
I appreciate all the love and support in my life.
Life is beautiful, and I am a part of it.
I enjoy the miracle that life is.
I appreciate and support the people in my life.
I love and care for myself and others.

Praying

Prayer is when we ask for help. This is a beautiful and powerful way to call on your own inner wisdom. The beautiful thing about prayer is that you can pray whenever, and wherever. Prayer can be a source of support, hope, and faith that things will work out for the best. Prayer can also help you unleash your inner guidance, and bring up exactly what you need to work on. There is no right or wrong way to pray. You don't even have to believe in a god to pray. Spirituality is non-denominational.

1. Make the right environment. The best place to pray is a quiet place where no one is there to disturb you.

2. Praise God or simply express gratitude for your life.

3. Ask for forgiveness if needed.

4. Decide what you want to pray about.

5. Pray for blessings. Ask for help.

6. Thank God, a higher power, or the universe.

7. Pray in a way that feels natural to you.

Gratitude Journal

Gratitude is the quality of being thankful. It is a wonderful way to return kindness to others by showing your appreciation for what and who they are. A daily practice of gratitude is a wonderful way to form the habit of appreciation. Gratitude is simply being very thankful and appreciative for all that has come into your life! When you are feeling down, one of the best things you can do is practice expressing gratitude or journal all that you are grateful for. What you put your attention on is really what you will be noticing and will create your reality. During difficult times and in emotions such as sadness, anxiety, and worry, it is harder to express gratitude, but it is actually the most essential time to be grateful. One of the best ways to get into the habit of expressing gratitude is to repeat the practice every day. Pick a time of day, and commit to the practice of journalling your gratitude. One of the best times is just before bed at the end of the day. Concluding your day with what you are grateful for, allows you to appreciate your day.

1. Start by selecting a nice-looking journal that excites you. Make it so you LOVE your journal.

2. Plan a place and time to write in your journal. Think about something that is already a habit for you and add the practice of writing in your journal to that habit. Repeat consistently. Commit to writing in your journal for a period of time.

3. Start writing. Do not worry about the content or if you are doing it right or wrong; simply write out things from your day that you are grateful for or that you appreciated. You can do your journal in bullet points, sentences, or any way that makes you feel good. This is a chance to celebrate your day.

Reflection

What was your biggest discovery through this step?

How are you going to bring this practice into your life?

How will this contribute to your life?

9

Resilience & Strength

"Resilience is knowing that you are the only one that has the power and the responsibility to pick yourself up."

-Mary Holloway

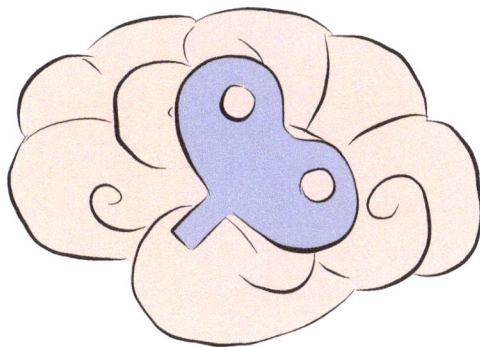

Resilience and Strength

What is resilience?

When faced with adversity in life, how does a person cope or adapt? Why do some people seem to bounce back from tragic events or loss much more quickly than others? Why do some people seem to get "stuck" in a point in their life, without the ability to move forward? Psychologists have long studied these issues, and have come up with a label you may be familiar with: resilience. Resilience is how well a person can adapt to events in their life, such as when faced with a tragedy, natural disaster, health concern, relationship issue, work problem, or school trouble. A person with good resilience has the ability to bounce back more quickly and with less stress than someone whose resilience is less developed. Resilience is what gives people the psychological strength to cope with stress and hardship. It is the mental reservoir of strength that people are able to call on in times of need to carry them through without falling apart. Psychologists believe that resilient individuals are better able to handle adversity and rebuild their lives after a catastrophe. Dealing with change or loss is an inevitable part of life. At some point, everyone experiences setbacks of varying degrees. How we deal with these problems can play a significant role in not only the outcome, but also the long-term psychological consequences.

Why is resilience important?

Being resilient is about being able to adapt and bounce back in the face of challenges. Challenges will occur in our lives, so it is important to learn the tools and skills needed to cope with struggle. For researchers and professionals, resilience is not just about bouncing back; it's about bouncing forward. Resilience doesn't just mean getting back to normal after facing a difficult situation; it means learning from the process in order to become stronger and better at tackling the next challenge. It's not limited to tragedies or major life events, either. Resilience applies to more common struggles too. In fact, when people respond to any type of challenge, it creates an opportunity to bounce forward. It helps them learn coping skills and find solutions to problems.

Perception Shift

The events and circumstances that we experience are all up to interpretation. It is how we perceive these events that determines whether we are suffering, or we are growing and learning. We have the choice as to how we interpret events. Our personal beliefs and stories along with our experiences, affect how we interpret or perceive events. One of the best ways to shift your perception is to look at challenges as opportunities to grow and change. By cultivating a growth mindset, you will become better at adapting to change and challenges. There are going to be ups and downs in life and it is through this practice that you can start to transform challenges, making any past and present challenges a more positive learning experience.

According to the Chopra Centre, you can take these FIVE STEPS TO TRANSFORM CHALLENGES INTO GIFTS:

Step 1: Ask yourself what just happened, without judgment or creating any story around it. Stick to the facts.

Step 2: Identify the emotions that are arising within you, and refrain from blaming another person or circumstance.

Step 3: Look at the big picture, and ask yourself if the situation realistically serves your highest purpose. Does the way that you are choosing to interpret your experience serve your highest purpose?

Step 4: Identify the lesson by looking for what could possibly be RIGHT about this situation, even though it is causing you pain at this moment.

Step 5: Once you've pinpointed the lesson, or the gift, you can consciously choose to interpret the circumstances through the lens of positivity. Identify a new way you can view the situation that supports and empowers you.

 As you practice these steps, you'll see how it is possible to shift from despair into a state of being where a whole new reality emerges. This is how you consciously co-create the life you want to be living.

"Taking time to do nothing often brings everything into perspective."

-Doe Zantamta

How Might I?

Every problem is an opportunity of developing more resilience. By framing your challenge as a "how might I" question, you'll set yourself up for an innovative solution.

Step 1: Identify problematic areas that could be a challenge to you.

Step 2: Try looking at each challenge by adding the question "how might I?" at the beginning. For example, you could ask: "How might I grow my business?"

Step 3: Take a look at your "how might I" question, and ask yourself if it allows for a variety of solutions. Your "how might I" should generate a number of possible options and can become a launch pad for your brainstorms.

Step 4: With a bunch of new options and a variety of solutions, you will feel more resilient and confident moving forward.

Reflection

What was your biggest discovery through this step?

How are you going to bring this practice into your life?

How will this contribute to your life?

10

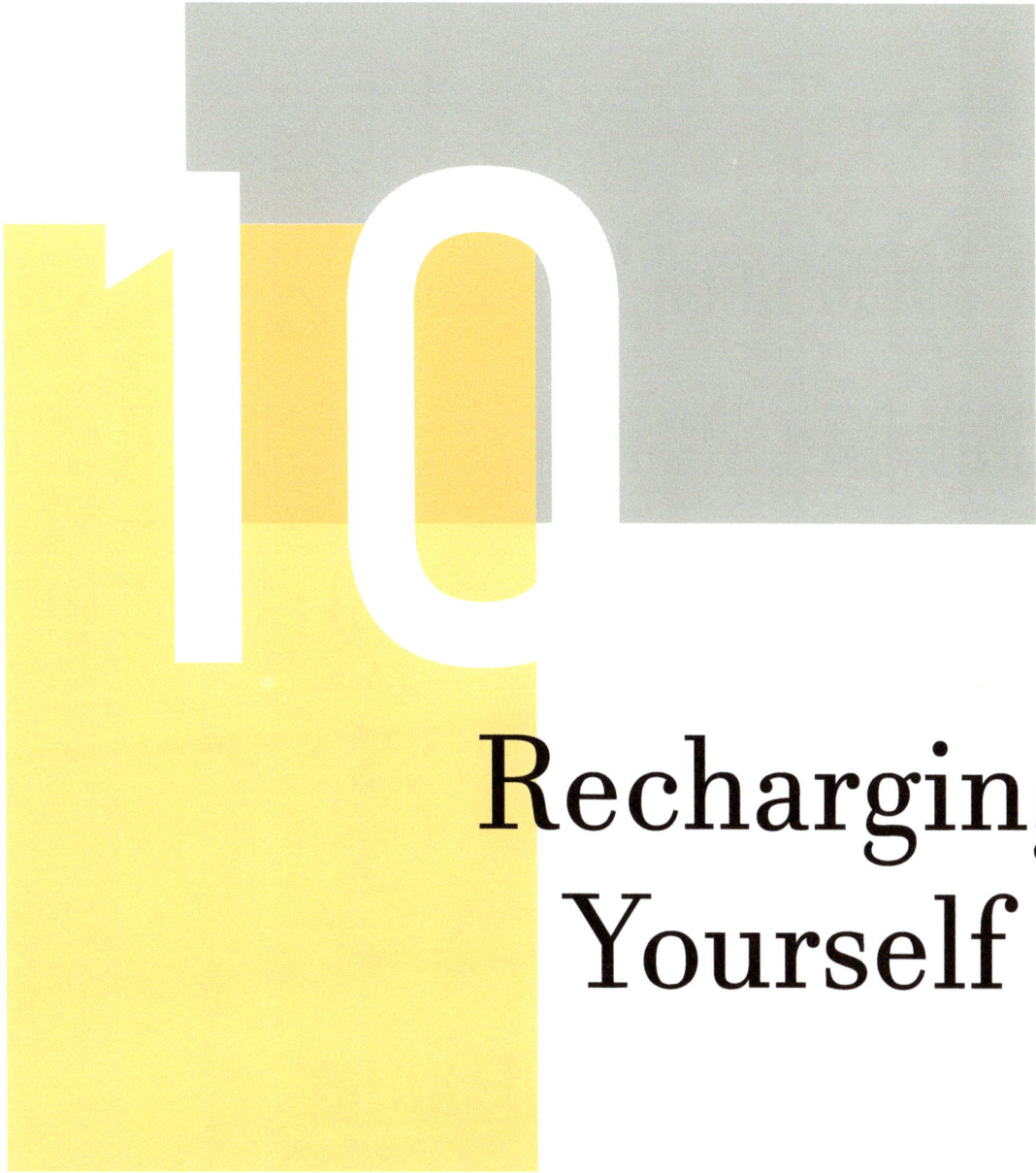

Recharging Yourself

"Sometimes we need to go off on our own. We're not sad. We're not angry. We just need to recharge our batteries ."

-Kristen Butler

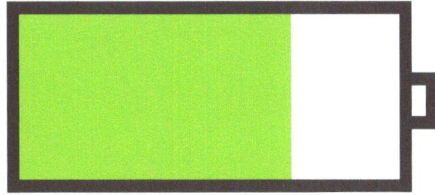

Recharging Yourself

You know that your phone has to go back onto recharge every night in order to work the next day. Our bodies also need to recharge and replenish in order to function. Self-care is a human form of recharging and building up strength again. Self-care can mean different things to different people, but we all need it in our everyday life. According to Psychologist Joseph Cardillo, Ph.D., a hallmark of body-energy management is that you happily flow from one activity to the next. Instead of feeling frazzled by what you do, you acquire more energy and more satisfaction. When these elements are in sync, each action, each day fuels the next. Good energy is having the right energy—physically and mentally—to fuel your actions throughout the day. The most common reason healthy people feel drained, stressed, and/or unable to get good sleep at night, is energy mismanagement. Here is proof that you should be taking time out of your day to rest and refresh:

It reduces stress: Have you ever noticed you are not yourself when you are frazzled or stressed out? That's because stress is when your brain thinks you are being threatened in some way, so your mind is not functioning properly. Stress shuts down our normal brain processes and ability to think logically, making us a person that isn't as pleasant to be around.

The stress hormone cortisol makes you feel panicked and on edge, but when you relax, you'll give your "feel-good" neuro-chemicals a chance to be released.

It increases creativity: When we are rested and replenished, we function at our best and everything in life seems to flow. We are more in tune with our inner voice, inner creativity, and we are able to flourish in our lives. By resting and recharging, you allow your best self to show up and you are able to balance your life. When you make time off just as important as time on, you will gain energy, focus and stamina to better manage your life. In his book, The 7 Habits of Highly Effective People, Stephen Covey explains the seventh habit by using the analogy of a woodcutter: A woodcutter had been sawing out in the woods for several days straight. As the days went by he noticed that his productivity was dropping. It was getting harder and harder to saw with each successive day. After all, the process of cutting dulls the blade. And, the duller the blade, the greater the effort that is required to keep sawing. The solution, of course, was for the woodcutter to stop periodically to sharpen the saw. In much the same way, you can take steps to prevent burnout and to maintain peak performance by sharpening the saw. When you make time off as important as time on, and have a plan to use it effectively, you gain the skill of energy management.

Energy Inventory

Identifying your own energy traps and mismatches, and replacing them with the right energy, will plug your energy drains and increase your energy gains. You will get more done with less effort and greater satisfaction when you can train your body and mind to operate with "higher-quality currency."

What typically drains your energy?

What is an energy drain in your day?

When do you have energy dips?

What typically increases your energy?

What gives you a burst of energy in your day?

When do you have an energy increase or surge?

"Be strong enough to stand alone, smart enough to know when you need help, and brave enough to ask for it."

-Ziad K. Abdelnour

Your Own Way to Recharge

Here are some suggestions as to how you can recharge:

Set aside one day a week to fully rest. Lazy Sundays are perfect. Turn off your Wi-Fi temporarily. Go to the spa. Pamper yourself. No Internet means no social media. Shut down your cell phone. Take a relaxing bath. Request a mental health day. Light a candle. Go into nature. Most bosses are more than happy to give you a day off work for the sake of mental health. Take a vacation. Meditate; even a few minutes can do wonders. Take a nap. Take a drive. Walk your dog. Colour. Get some sun. Breathe fresh air. Take a technology break. Read a book. Journal. Get a pedicure. Do a nutritional cleanse. Exercise. Walk daily. Go to a retreat. Do yoga. Try a new class. Create a not-to-do list. Now, think of your own...

What methods of recharging resonates with you the most?

What are you going to do to recharge today?

What are you going to plan for this week to recharge?

What are you going to plan for the next month to recharge?

Energy Hacks

Joseph Cardillo, Ph.D., is an expert on energy teaching and in his book Body Intelligence: Harness Your Body's Energy for Your Best Life, he makes the following suggestions for instant energy:

1. Heighten your energy with this one-two punch: Find an environmental photo that has a relaxing effect on you and a piece of fast-paced music that makes your energy soar. Place these on your cell phone. Relax and deepen your breathing, empty your mind of thoughts, and mindfully observe the photo for five to seven minutes. Afterward, play your fast tune. This combo quadruples your energy. Alternately, use your relaxing photo in combination with slower music and soothing lyrics to lower energy when needed. Listen for 12 minutes.

2. Eliminate burnout: Don't surrender. Instead, switch activities to something more rewarding and pile it on, pushing the pedal to the metal until you recharge. You'll reset the electrical activity in your mind and body, and enjoy a cascade of self-produced anti-stress and happy hormones. Always have an awesome long-term sideline project you can shift to for a while.

3. Massage this acupoint to bust stress: In a seated position and well postured, as if there is a string atop your head pulling upward, use your thumb to gently rub the bottom (center) of each foot. It works fast.

4. Change mental frequencies to eliminate bad moods: Put a photo of a loved one, friend or pet doing something positive and silly (the sillier the better) on your phone. Making those childish funny faces or facial expressions works great.

5. Plan a recharging activity: Think over tomorrow's agenda. Identify a predictable situation that will potentially drain a lot of energy. Plan a restorative activity before or after. Get to a different environment and do something creative: Listen to an audiobook, sketch a natural scene, try some creative writing. Go slow. Fuel your spirit, restore your energy and enjoy.

"Be strong enough to stand alone, smart enough to know when you need help, and brave enough to ask for it."

-Ziad K. Abdelnour

Reflection

What was your biggest discovery through this step?

How are you going to bring this practice into your life?

How will this contribute to your life?

11

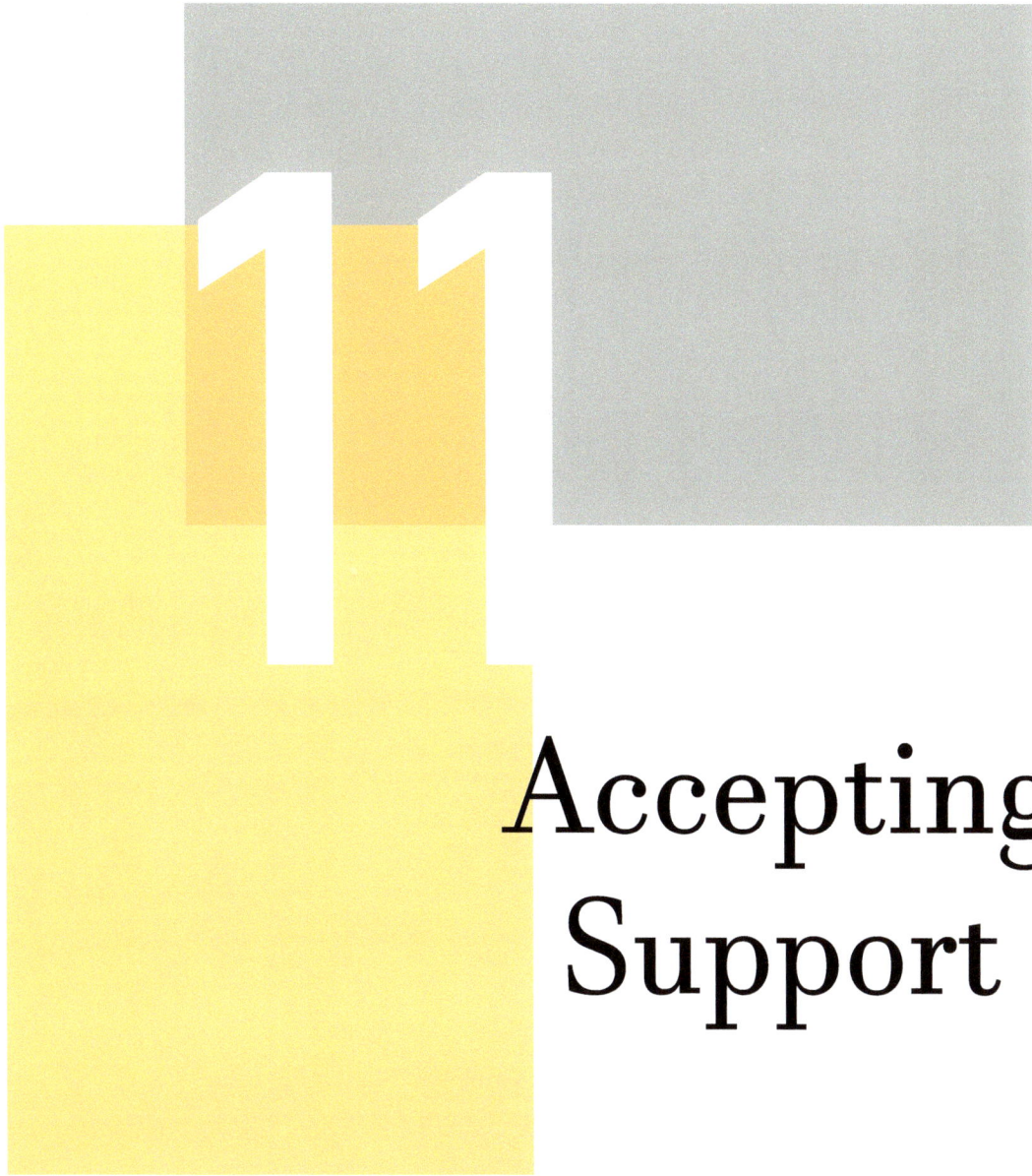

Accepting Support

"Sometimes I just want someone to hug me and say, I know it's hard, but you're going to be okay."

-Unknown

Accepting Support

How can help benefit your life?

Do you ever feel overwhelmed, stressed, and out of energy? At times it's really hard to ask for help. We often think that asking for help makes us look weak, uncertain, and unable. It can be a bit of a challenge for some people to ask for support, but asking for support can be one of the best ways to look after yourself.

It is important to acknowledge that we can do everything ourselves, that we are human, and at times we need support. But sometimes we all could really benefit from added support. The actual act of asking for help can be challenging, but you have to remember it will make you stronger in the end.

You have probably heard the popular African proverb, "It takes a village to raise a child." What this proverb actually means is that the work of raising a child cannot be done alone; rather, an entire community must participate to some extent for the best possible outcome.

Asking for support can actually produce better outcomes, make you more productive, and facilitate self-care.

Be sure to maintain an awareness as to when you need help and support, then be open to receiving help.

There are many benefits to asking for support:

- You will maintain your own energy.
- You can share the task and pressure.
- You allow others to be kind.
- You are offering trust and friendship.
- You are acknowledging that you are human.
- You are co-creating your life

Your Support System

Make your list: Take this time to identify the people who are always there for you. Also think of the people who would be there for you if you simply asked. There will always be good and bad days; it is important to remember the people that you can call on during these challenges and also successes. Through it all, we do need support. At this point it's important to figure out what support means to you. When you hear the words "help" or "support," what comes to mind for you? Look at it this way: Support can mean anything that is going to lift you up and make you feel better. Anything that will assist you, encourage you and boost you up.

Write your insight here...

Make Your List Here....

What makes up your support system? There are many ways you can be supported. Come up with your own list of methods of help that will support you and offer self-care. Anything or anyone that can bring you comfort and self-soothing. Some examples might be: professionals like coaches, counsellors, therapists, friends and family, special places like churches, parks, hiking trails, reading chairs, coffee shops, nice environments (like those with calm music, candles and incense) yoga studios, clean spaces, walking outdoors, petting dogs, etc. Now make your own list of things that make you feel safe and comfortable.

What makes up your
Support System?

Clarify the support you need.

When you are present and open, you will be more likely to notice what you're feeling, what you're thinking, and what you might need.

You can practice mindfully opening to what your needs are by:

Step 1: Taking a moment to breathe with awareness, noticing what your body and mind might be telling you.

Step 2: Pausing for a moment to reflect on what you might be needing support with. Ask yourself what is particularly challenging right now?

Step 3: Taking an inventory of your needs. Ask yourself:
Am I satisfied with the quality of my life?
Do I have adequate opportunity to exercise my strengths?
Do I have autonomy in my day-to-day life decisions?
Am I struggling with something in particular?
What would help me?
What am I in need of?
What would make me feel better?

Step 4: Take notes of any ideas or resources you can draw on. Isolate the things that could offer you support.

Reflection

What was your biggest discovery through this step?

How are you going to bring this practice into your life?

How will this contribute to your life?

12

Savouring and Life Joy

"Find joy in the ordinary."

-Unknown

Savouring and Life Joy

One of the best ways to feel more positive emotions is to know there is beauty all around you that should be savoured at all moments. All too often we become busy and go on automatic pilot, while we are surrounded by so much joy and beauty. Savouring is one of the best ways to really absorb life joy. We can even savour moments that have passed, moments that we are in, and forthcoming exciting moments for the future. Savouring is one of the best tools to enhance positive emotions.

All you have to do is adopt a practice of savouring. By celebrating all these tiny moments instead of letting them fade too quickly, we can enhance our level of happiness. Savoring is all about fully feeling, enjoying, and elongating our positive experiences. We all want our positive moments to be long-lasting and offer us a steady stream of positive thoughts and emotions. Savouring is the best way to do this.

It is essentially making the good times stick in our brains longer. In the world of positive psychology, savouring is best described by the model created by Fred Bryant and Joseph Veroff.

This model defines savouring as "noticing and appreciating the positive aspects of life." "Savouring is more than pleasure; it also involves mindfulness and conscious attention to the experience of pleasure." How can we learn to savour, and use it to our advantage? Fred Bryant and Joseph Veroff describe how this process works by locking us into the moment through our state of mind and attention.

What is needed to savour an experience in a positive way is to engage fully in the experience and be conscious and mindful of every detail you can take in, and to wholly appreciate it. Dr. Martin Seligman, the father of positive psychology, suggests an idea of happiness as supported by mindfulness and savouring, describing savouring as the awareness of pleasure as it occurs. He calls for mindful, conscious attention to the experience and how pleasure is derived from that.

Practicing the technique of savouring intensifies and lengthens positive emotion. That makes for wonderful days and afterglows of life joy!

"Stop for a breath; come up for air. Give yourself permission to enjoy the moment. The finish line will still be there tomorrow."

-Unknown

1. Start making a list of all the simple things that bring you pleasure.

2. Make another list with all the things that you think would bring you pleasure and happiness.

3. Make arrangements in your schedule to add the things that bring you pleasure on a daily basis.

4. Make arrangements in your schedule to add the bigger things that would bring you pleasure and happiness.

5. Make another list that highlights the things you find negative, annoying or frustrating.

6. Decide which things you can remove from your life.

7. Review your list often. Add things that bring you pleasure.

8. Savour all the things that bring you pleasure and that you are grateful for!

Do what gives you

pleasure.

Savour The Past

Savouring the past is a good start to practicing savouring.

Step 1: Spend a few minutes thinking about a happy, joyful, or pleasant experience that happened to you in the last month.

Step 2: As you are thinking back on the good experience, think about every aspect of that experience. Smells, sights, sounds and sensations

Step 3: Really let your mind go off and enjoy every aspect of that experience. Let your thoughts wander to anything else about the experience that makes you feel good.

Step 4: Mentally hold onto everything that feels good. Try it. Journal what comes up for you. Make a list of past events that you can bring up and try to savour them often!

 Draw on your list any time. Talk about happy positive past moments often!

Savour the Present

I'm sure you've heard the expression "stop and smell the roses." Science has shown that when we stop and appreciate all the small and simple pleasures that life has to offer, we will be happier. When you find yourself feeling happy and good, try to mentally hold onto that feeling as long as you can. Pay really close attention and be mindful in the moments that feel good.

Here are some ways you can savour the present moment:
Gratitude: Take the time to be grateful for all the good things in your life. When you do this, you experience the positive emotions that go along with the good things. Gratitude and appreciation are wonderful tools to help you savour the present moment

Positive emotions: Try to extend the length of time you feel positive emotions. When you feel good, be sure to talk about it, share it with other people, and think about it a lot. Keep those positive emotions at the front of your mind.

Savour the future: Take time to think about exciting fun things that you would love to have happen in your future. Think about how you would feel if you were to achieve those things. Make sure that this future thinking generates positive emotions.

"Only those who have learned the power of sincere and selfless contribution experience life's deepest joy: true fulfillment."

- Tony Robbins

Reflection

What was your biggest discovery through this step?

How are you going to bring this practice into your life?

How will this contribute to your life?

References and Resources

Brown, Brené (2012): Daring Greatly: How the Courage to Be Vulnerable Transforms the Way We Live, Love, Parent, and Lead. New York City, NY: Gotham.

Bryant, Fred B. and Veroff, Joseph (2007): Savoring: A New Model of Positive Experience. Lawrence Erlbaum Associates Publishers.

Cole, Steve: Professor of Medicine and Psychiatry and Biobehavioral Sciences at the UCLA School of Medicine.

Covey, Stephen Richards (1989): The 7 Habits of Highly Effective People. Free Press.

Duhigg, Charles (2012): The Power of Habit: Why We Do What We Do in Life and Business. Random House.

Gottman, John, Ph.D. and Silver, Nan (1999): The Seven Principles for Making Marriage Work. New York, NY: Three Rivers Press.

Lyubomirsky, Sonja. (2008) The How of Happiness: A Scientific Approach to Getting the Life You Want. Penguin Press.

Pennebaker, James W.: Social psychologist and Professor at the University of Texas at Austin.

Seligman, Martin Elias Peter "Marty", Ph.D.: Author of numerous self-help books and Professor of Psychology at the University of Pennsylvania.

Seppälä, Emma, Ph.D. (2016): The Happiness Track. HarperOne.

About the Author:

As a certified, positive-psychology practitioner and life coach, I have changed my life through discovering some powerful tools and strategies that anyone can apply to their lives. I make no secret of the fact that this discovery has truly saved me. Therefore, I have now made it my personal mission to help others follow their passion, discover their dream job, and live a healthy life. As a health-and-habit coach, I am taking all of my learnings and devoting my career to supporting others in their journey to find their potential. As a mother and wife, I went from being a victim to being a victor. You can too!

To find out more about Saghar Alavi's coaching services and programs go to www.Happylifestyle.ca

Photo by Elham Karimian

www.ingramcontent.com/pod-product-compliance
Lightning Source LLC
Chambersburg PA
CBHW060808270326

41928CB00002B/27